I0490809

MASTERING BITCOIN

A Comprehensive Guide to Cryptocurrency Investing and Trading

Philipp Frühwirth

CONTENTS

INTRODUCTION: WHAT IS BITCOIN AND HOW DOES IT WORK?

Ever since its introduction in 2009, Bitcoin has taken the world by storm. This digital currency has revolutionized the way we think about money and what it means to be a store of value. Unlike traditional currencies such as the U.S. dollar or the euro, Bitcoin operates in a decentralized system, meaning it does not rely on any single institution or government for its value or legitimacy.

So, what exactly is Bitcoin and how does it work? At its core, Bitcoin is a digital currency, also known as a cryptocurrency, which operates on a decentralized ledger called the blockchain. It was created by an unknown individual or group who went by the pseudonym Satoshi Nakamoto, and its purpose was to provide a decentralized alternative to the traditional banking system.

The blockchain is essentially a publicly accessible digital ledger that records all Bitcoin transactions. This means that every transaction made with Bitcoin is publicly visible and can be verified by anyone on the network. The blockchain is maintained by a network of nodes, or computers, which work together to validate new transactions and update the ledger accordingly.

One of the most unique features of Bitcoin is the process of mining. Mining is the process of using powerful computing hardware to solve complex mathematical problems, which are used to validate transactions and add them to the blockchain. Miners are incentivized to participate in this process by receiving Bitcoin as a reward for their efforts.

Once a transaction has been added to the blockchain, it cannot be reversed or altered, which makes the system incredibly secure and resistant to fraud. This has made Bitcoin an attractive option for people who are concerned about the security and privacy of their financial transactions.

Bitcoin has gained popularity over the years for a variety of reasons. Firstly, it offers a low-cost and efficient way to transfer funds across borders without the need for a bank or other intermediary. This has made it particularly popular in countries with less stable financial systems, where people may not trust banks or governments with their money.

Another reason for Bitcoin's popularity is its limited supply. There will never be more than 21 million Bitcoins in existence, which means that unlike traditional currencies, it is not subject to inflation. This makes Bitcoin an attractive option for people who are looking for a stable store of value.

In conclusion, Bitcoin is a groundbreaking digital currency that operates on a decentralized system. It is maintained by a network of nodes and uses mining to validate transactions and add them to a publicly accessible ledger called the blockchain. Its unique features have made it an attractive option for people who are looking for a secure and efficient way to transfer money without the need for intermediaries.

THE HISTORY OF BITCOIN: WHERE DID IT ALL BEGIN?

Bitcoin, the world's first decentralized digital currency, was introduced to the world in 2008 by a mysterious person or group of people who used the pseudonym "Satoshi Nakamoto." Its purpose was to create a new currency that would operate outside of the traditional banking system.

The first block of the Bitcoin blockchain was mined on January 3, 2009, which marked the beginning of the Bitcoin network. This first block, known as the "genesis block," had the message "The Times 03/Jan/2009 Chancellor on brink of second bailout for banks" embedded in it. This was a reference to a headline from the newspaper on that date, and it was seen as a jab at the traditional financial system.

Over the years, Bitcoin has gone through several phases of growth and development. In the early days, it was mainly used by tech enthusiasts and early adopters. However, as the currency grew in popularity, its use expanded to include more mainstream businesses and individuals.

In 2010, the first real-world Bitcoin transaction took place when a programmer named Laszlo Hanyecz bought two pizzas for 10,000 BTC. This transaction, which would be worth millions of dollars today, highlighted the potential of Bitcoin in everyday commerce.

In 2013, Bitcoin reached new heights in terms of valuation, with the currency briefly hitting $1,000 per Bitcoin. However, it soon experienced a sharp decline in value, and by 2015, it was hovering around $200 per BTC.

Throughout its history, Bitcoin has been associated with

controversy and speculation. In 2014, one of the largest Bitcoin exchanges at the time, Mt. Gox, filed for bankruptcy after it was revealed that the company had lost 850,000 BTC (then worth around $500 million) in a hacking attack. Other major exchanges have been hacked as well, leading some to question the security of the Bitcoin network.

Despite these challenges, Bitcoin has continued to gain acceptance and has proven to be a viable alternative to traditional currencies. The currency has attracted a dedicated community of developers, businesses, and enthusiasts who are working to make Bitcoin more accessible and useful to the world. Today, Bitcoin is increasingly being recognized as a legitimate form of money and a valuable asset for investment.

THE BASIC CONCEPTS OF BITCOIN: BLOCKCHAIN AND MINING

Bitcoin, at its core, is a decentralized digital currency that can be used for transactions worldwide. The revolutionary technology behind bitcoin is the blockchain, a distributed public ledger that records all transactions on the bitcoin network.

Blockchain technology enables secure, transparent, and tamper-proof transactions without requiring the involvement of a third party like a bank or government. This peer-to-peer trustless infrastructure allows bitcoin users to transfer funds directly to each other without the need for a middleman.

The blockchain is a network of computers called nodes, which work together to validate and verify transactions. Each node in the network stores a copy of the blockchain, which is constantly updated and synchronized with other nodes in real-time.

When a bitcoin transaction occurs, it is broadcast to the entire network of nodes. These nodes use complex algorithms to verify the transaction and ensure that the spender has the necessary funds to perform the transaction. Once the transaction has been verified, it is added to the blockchain, and a new block of transactions is created.

Mining, the process by which new bitcoins are created, is an essential part of the blockchain process. Miners use powerful computers to solve complex mathematical problems, and when they successfully complete a block of transactions, they are rewarded with newly minted bitcoins.

The process of mining involves verifying transactions and adding them to the blockchain while also serving as a Bitcoin network security system. The network of nodes forms a consensus about which transactions are valid and added to a new block. To add a block, miners must solve a cryptographic puzzle using their computing power. When they solve the puzzle, they are rewarded with a predetermined amount of newly created bitcoins.

The mining process ensures the integrity of the blockchain network by preventing fraudulent transactions and double-spending. The amount of new bitcoins created through the mining process is also limited, with a maximum of 21 million being created. This characteristic makes bitcoin a deflationary currency and one of the main factors that make it so valuable.

In summary, the blockchain and mining are the basic concepts that underpin the bitcoin network. These mechanisms ensure that transactions are secure, transparent, and tamper-proof. As the bitcoin network and other blockchain-based systems continue to evolve, these concepts will remain integral to understanding how the system operates.

THE DIFFERENT TYPES OF BITCOIN WALLETS AND HOW TO CHOOSE THE RIGHT ONE

Once you have purchased your first Bitcoin, the next step is finding a safe place to store it. Bitcoin wallets are digital wallets that allow you to store, send and receive Bitcoins. But with so many wallets available, choosing the right one can be a daunting task. In this chapter, we will explore the different types of Bitcoin wallets and help you decide which one is the best fit for you.

1. Hardware Wallets
Hardware wallets are physical devices that store your Bitcoins on a USB-like device. They are considered the most secure because they are offline and can only be accessed when plugged into a computer. The popular hardware wallets are Ledger Nano S, Trezor, and KeepKey.

2. Desktop Wallets
Desktop wallets allow you to store your Bitcoins on your computer. The security of desktop wallets depends on the user's expertise in computer security. If the computer is not secure, the wallet can be hacked. Electrum, Bitcoin Core and Exodus are popular desktop wallets.

3. Mobile Wallets
Mobile wallets are digital wallets that allow you to store Bitcoins on your mobile device. They are convenient for making payments on-the-go. However, they are more vulnerable to security threats and attacks. Mycelium, Bread, and Copay are popular mobile wallets.

4. Web Wallets

Web wallets allow you to store your Bitcoins online. They are convenient for making payments and accessible from any device with an internet connection. However, there is a risk of losing your Bitcoins if the wallet provider goes offline or is hacked. Coinbase, Blockchain.info, and Xapo are popular web wallets.

5. Paper Wallets

Paper wallets are physical copies of your public and private keys printed on a piece of paper. They offer a high level of security, as they are not connected to the internet. To use your Bitcoins, you need to import your private key to a software wallet. However, if the paper gets lost, you lose your Bitcoins forever.

When choosing a Bitcoin wallet, it is important to consider the level of security and convenience that you need. Hardware wallets are the safest option, but they can be expensive. Desktop and paper wallets offer a higher level of security than mobile and web wallets but can be less convenient. Mobile and web wallets are convenient, but they have a higher risk of being hacked.

It is also important to research the reputation and reviews of different wallets before choosing one. Consider factors such as customer support, user interface, and additional features such as 2-factor authentication.

In summary, choosing the right Bitcoin wallet is crucial to the security of your Bitcoins. By understanding the different types of wallets and their pros and cons, you can make an informed decision that suits your needs.

HOW TO BUY AND SELL BITCOIN: EXCHANGE PLATFORMS AND MARKETPLACES

Buying and selling Bitcoin is a relatively easy process, provided you have the right platforms and knowledge. Several platforms allow users to buy or sell Bitcoin and other cryptocurrencies. These include centralized exchanges, peer-to-peer exchanges, and marketplaces.

Centralized Exchanges

Centralized exchanges are online platforms that allow users to buy and sell cryptocurrencies in exchange for fiat currency (USD, EUR, GBP, etc.) or other cryptocurrencies. These exchanges are often run by a company or organization that acts as an intermediary between buyers and sellers.

Some of the popular centralized exchanges include Coinbase, Binance, Kraken, and Bitstamp. To use a centralized exchange, you will need to create an account, undergo a verification process, and link your bank account or credit card to your account. Once your account is set up, you can fund your account and start buying or selling Bitcoin.

Peer-to-Peer Exchanges

Peer-to-peer exchanges operate differently from centralized exchanges. They allow users to buy and sell Bitcoin directly from each other, bypassing the need for a centralized intermediary. This means that buyers and sellers can negotiate the price and terms of the transaction.

Some peer-to-peer exchanges include LocalBitcoins, Paxful, and Bisq. To use a peer-to-peer exchange, you will need to create an account, find a seller or buyer, and initiate the transaction. Peer-to-peer exchanges often have different payment options and support a wide range of fiat currencies.

Marketplaces

Marketplaces are similar to peer-to-peer exchanges in that they allow buyers and sellers to connect directly. However, marketplaces go beyond just buying and selling Bitcoin. They also offer other services such as escrow, cold storage, and merchant solutions.

Some marketplaces include OpenBazaar, Bitify, and Marketplace.tf. To use a marketplace, you will need to create an account, browse the available listings, and initiate the transaction. Marketplaces have various payment options and support a wide range of cryptocurrencies.

Conclusion

Buying and selling Bitcoin can seem like a daunting task, but with the right platforms and knowledge, it can be easy. Users can choose from centralized exchanges, peer-to-peer exchanges, and marketplaces based on their preference and needs. Always remember to do your research and choose a reputable platform to ensure a safe and secure transaction.

THE PROS AND CONS OF INVESTING IN BITCOIN

Bitcoin is a digital asset that is used as a medium of exchange for goods and services. As with any investment, there are pros and cons to consider before investing in Bitcoin. In this chapter, we will discuss the advantages and potential drawbacks of investing in Bitcoin.

Pros of Investing in Bitcoin

1. High Potential for Returns: Bitcoin's value has increased significantly in the past decade, making early investors very wealthy. This potential for high returns is a major draw for investors.

2. Decentralized System: The decentralized nature of Bitcoin means that it operates independently of any government or financial institution. This makes it appealing to those who value independence and freedom from traditional financial systems.

3. Great Liquidity: Since Bitcoin is a global currency, it is easy to buy and sell quickly, with no additional fees or wait times.

4. Anonymity: Transactions made with Bitcoin can be anonymous, which means that investors have more privacy and control over their money.

5. Increasing Acceptance: Bitcoin's acceptance has increased significantly over the years, with more and more merchants accepting it as a form of payment.

Cons of Investing in Bitcoin

1. High Volatility: Bitcoin has a reputation for being highly

volatile, with price fluctuations that can be unpredictable. This can be a disadvantage for investors who prefer stability in their investments.

2. Security Risks: In the past, there have been several large-scale hacks resulting in the loss of Bitcoin. Investors must be cautious and take steps to protect their investments, such as using secure wallets and two-factor authentication.

3. Regulatory Risks: Bitcoin is not regulated by any centralized authority, leaving it vulnerable to regulatory changes that can affect its value and legality.

4. Lack of Fundamental Value: Some investors argue that Bitcoin lacks fundamental value, unlike stocks or real estate. This means that its value is based on speculation and hype, which can be a disadvantage for investors seeking long-term, stable investments.

5. Competition from Other Cryptocurrencies: Bitcoin is not the only cryptocurrency available for investment. It competes with other cryptocurrencies, some of which offer different features and benefits, making it challenging to know which one will be the most successful in the future.

Conclusion

Investing in Bitcoin can be a high-risk, high-reward endeavor. Before investing in Bitcoin, it is essential to research the market and evaluate the pros and cons carefully. Investors must also be mindful of security risks and regulatory changes that can affect their investments. Ultimately, investing in Bitcoin requires a deep understanding of the market and the willingness to accept the potential risks involved.

UNDERSTANDING THE RISKS ASSOCIATED WITH BITCOIN: SECURITY THREATS AND SCAMS

As with any form of digital payment, Bitcoin carries certain risks that users should be aware of. While the blockchain technology that powers Bitcoin is extremely secure, there are still potential security threats and scams that users need to be wary of.

One of the most common forms of Bitcoin scams is phishing attacks. Phishing attacks can come in many forms, but they all share the same goal – to trick users into giving away their private keys or login credentials. These attacks can be carried out through email, social media, or even fake websites that look like legitimate Bitcoin services.

Another potential security risk is the use of poorly-secured Bitcoin wallets. Bitcoin wallets can be stored online or offline, and both types of wallets have their own risks. Online wallets are vulnerable to hacking attacks, while offline wallets can be lost or stolen.

In addition to security risks, there are also other potential drawbacks to investing in Bitcoin. One of the biggest drawbacks is the high volatility of the Bitcoin market. The price of Bitcoin has been known to fluctuate wildly, sometimes experiencing sudden drops or spikes in value. This volatility can make it difficult to predict the future value of Bitcoin, which can be a concern for investors.

Another potential risk of investing in Bitcoin is the lack of regulation in the market. While governments around the world have been starting to take a closer look at Bitcoin in recent years, there is still no universal regulation in place. This lack of oversight can make it easier for scammers and fraudsters to take advantage of unsuspecting investors.

Despite these risks, many investors still see Bitcoin as a worthy investment opportunity. The decentralized nature of Bitcoin makes it resistant to government control and inflation, and the underlying blockchain technology has a wide range of potential applications beyond just digital currency.

Ultimately, whether or not to invest in Bitcoin will depend on your individual risk tolerance and investment goals. While Bitcoin does carry certain risks, it also has the potential for significant rewards for those who are willing to take the plunge. Just be sure to do your research and take steps to safeguard your investments to minimize your risk exposure.

THE LEGAL IMPLICATIONS OF BITCOIN: REGULATIONS AND TAXATION

As with any financial product or asset, Bitcoin is subject to laws and regulations that govern its use and taxation. Understanding these laws and regulations is crucial for anyone wishing to engage in Bitcoin-related activities, such as buying, selling, holding, or investing.

Regulations

Governments around the world have varying regulations when it comes to Bitcoin. In the United States, for example, the Financial Crimes Enforcement Network (FinCEN) has issued guidelines for Bitcoin exchanges and other businesses dealing in virtual currency. These guidelines require Bitcoin businesses to register with FinCEN and comply with anti-money laundering (AML) and know-your-customer (KYC) requirements.

Other countries, such as Japan and Australia, have also introduced regulations aimed at combating money laundering and ensuring the safety of consumers. However, the approach varies between countries and there is no universally accepted regulatory framework for Bitcoin.

Taxation

Another important consideration when it comes to Bitcoin is taxation. In the United States, Bitcoin and other cryptocurrencies are treated as property for tax purposes. This means that any gains or losses from selling, trading, or using Bitcoin are subject to capital gains tax.

The tax rate depends on various factors, including the holding period, the taxpayer's income, and the taxpayer's tax bracket. It's important to consult with a tax professional to understand the tax implications of Bitcoin transactions and to ensure compliance with the relevant laws and regulations.

Choosing the right country and jurisdiction for engaging in Bitcoin activities can also have tax implications. For example, some countries have more favorable tax laws for Bitcoin transactions than others.

Conclusion

Bitcoin is a relatively new asset class and as such, the legal and regulatory landscape is still evolving. It's important for anyone considering engaging in Bitcoin-related activities to educate themselves on the laws and regulations in their jurisdiction, as well as the tax implications. Failing to comply with the relevant laws and regulations could result in fines, penalties, or even legal action.

BITCOIN TRANSACTIONS: HOW TO SEND AND RECEIVE PAYMENTS

Bitcoin transactions are at the heart of the cryptocurrency's technology. This chapter will guide you through the process of how to send and receive bitcoin payments.

To send a Bitcoin payment, you will need a Bitcoin wallet and the recipient's wallet information. You can send Bitcoin from your wallet by entering the amount you want to send and the recipient's Bitcoin address. Once you click "send," the transaction will be broadcasted to the Bitcoin network.

To receive a Bitcoin payment, the process is just as simple. You will need to share your Bitcoin address with the sender. This address can be found in your Bitcoin wallet under the "receive" section. Once you have received payment, the transaction will be verified and added to the Bitcoin network's blockchain.

It's important to note that Bitcoin transactions can take anywhere from several minutes to several hours to complete. This is because each transaction must be validated by the network's miners before it is added to the blockchain. Additionally, the speed of transactions can be affected by the current network congestion and transaction fees.

Transaction fees are paid by the sender to the network's miners to incentivize them to validate the transaction quickly. These fees can vary depending on the current demand for transactions and the size of the transaction.

It's also important to take precautions to ensure your transaction is secure. You should always double-check the Bitcoin address you are sending payment to ensure it is accurate. Additionally, you should never share your private key with anyone as this can allow them to access your Bitcoin wallet and steal your funds.

Finally, it's important to keep track of your Bitcoin transactions for tax purposes. In the United States, Bitcoin transactions are subject to capital gains tax. This means that if you sell Bitcoin for a profit, you will need to report that income on your tax return.

In conclusion, Bitcoin transactions are a fundamental aspect of the cryptocurrency's technology. By following the steps outlined in this chapter, you can send and receive Bitcoin payments with relative ease.

THE FUTURE OF BITCOIN: PREDICTIONS AND SPECULATIONS

Since its creation, Bitcoin has been a topic of debate among finance experts, governments, and regulators. While some consider it to be the future of money, others believe it to be a bubble that will eventually burst. So, what does the future hold for Bitcoin? Here are some predictions and speculations:

1. Bitcoin Will See More Adoption: Bitcoin's adoption rate has been growing steadily, and this trend is expected to continue. More and more businesses are accepting Bitcoin payments, and major financial institutions are investing in blockchain technology. This increased adoption could lead to an increased demand for Bitcoin, and consequently, an increase in its value.

2. Bitcoin Could Replace Gold: Bitcoin is often compared to gold, given its scarcity and the fact that it can be used as a store of value. Some experts believe that Bitcoin could eventually replace gold as a store of value, especially given its convenience and ease of transfer.

3. Governments Will Regulate Bitcoin: As Bitcoin continues to gain popularity, governments and regulatory bodies are likely to step in to regulate it. This could lead to increased scrutiny and oversight, which could impact Bitcoin's value and adoption rate.

4. Bitcoin Could Face Technical Challenges: Bitcoin's scalability and transaction speed have been major points of concern for some time, and these issues could become more pronounced as adoption rates increase. If these challenges are not addressed, they could limit Bitcoin's growth potential.

5. Bitcoin Could Face Competition: While Bitcoin is currently the most popular cryptocurrency, it may not remain so forever. Other cryptocurrencies, such as Ethereum and Litecoin, are gaining popularity and could potentially challenge Bitcoin's dominance.

6. Bitcoin Price Will Continue to Be Volatile: The price of Bitcoin has been volatile since its inception, and this is likely to continue. Factors such as regulatory changes, technical challenges, and market sentiment could all impact Bitcoin's value in the future.

Overall, the future of Bitcoin is difficult to predict with certainty. While some believe that it will continue to gain value and adoption, others believe that it is a bubble waiting to burst. Regardless of where Bitcoin is headed, it is clear that it will continue to generate debate and interest in the world of finance and beyond.

HOW TO ACCEPT BITCOIN PAYMENTS: A GUIDE FOR SMALL BUSINESS OWNERS

For small business owners, accepting different payment methods is essential to stay competitive and meet customer needs. One payment option that has gained popularity in recent years is Bitcoin. By accepting Bitcoin payments, a business can expand its customer base and potentially increase sales. However, for those unfamiliar with Bitcoin, the process of accepting payments can seem daunting. In this chapter, we will guide small business owners through the process of accepting Bitcoin payments, step by step.

The first step in accepting Bitcoin payments is to set up a Bitcoin wallet. This will allow customers to send Bitcoin payments to your business. There are multiple types of wallets available, including desktop wallets, mobile wallets, web wallets, and hardware wallets. As discussed in Chapter 4, it is important to choose the right type of wallet for your business based on factors such as security, ease of use, and accessibility.

Once you have set up a Bitcoin wallet, it is important to inform your customers that you now accept Bitcoin payments. You can do this by adding a Bitcoin payment option to your website, displaying a sign in your storefront or adding it to your payment options during checkout. Inform your customers of the benefits of using Bitcoin such as faster transactions, low fees, and increased privacy.

When a customer chooses to pay with Bitcoin, provide them with the wallet address to send the payment to. This address can be generated within your wallet software. It is important to ensure that the wallet address provided is accurate to avoid any errors in payment. Additionally, with Bitcoin, all transactions are public, which means that you or your customer can track the payment as it moves across the blockchain.

Once the payment is received, you will need to confirm the payment within your Bitcoin wallet software. The payment will then be added to your wallet balance. From there, you can choose to keep the Bitcoin as an investment or convert it to your local currency. Conversion can be done through an exchange that supports your local currency. However, it is important to note that you should weigh the pros and cons of holding Bitcoin versus selling it, as the value of Bitcoin can fluctuate significantly.

In conclusion, accepting Bitcoin payments can benefit small business owners by expanding the customer base and offering more payment options. By following the steps outlined in this chapter and ensuring proper wallet security protocols, small business owners can successfully accept Bitcoin payments and potentially increase sales.

BITCOIN MINING: HOW TO START YOUR OWN MINING RIG

Mining is an essential aspect of the Bitcoin network, as it is the process that validates transactions and the creation of new coins. For a long time, mining Bitcoin was possible using basic CPUs, but the computing power required has since increased drastically. Nowadays, specialized hardware called ASICs (Application-Specific Integrated Circuits) is necessary to mine Bitcoin in a productive way. In this chapter, we will cover the basics of Bitcoin mining and how to start your own mining rig.

Bitcoin mining is the process of validating transactions on the network by solving complex mathematical algorithms. These algorithms require a lot of computational power, which is provided by miners. Whenever a miner solves an algorithm, they are rewarded with a certain amount of Bitcoin, making mining a potentially profitable endeavor.

To start mining Bitcoin, you will need to have a powerful mining rig. While it is possible to mine Bitcoin using a regular computer or laptop, the low hash rate of these devices will make it hard to earn any meaningful rewards. The bare minimum you will need to get started is an ASIC mining rig, which is a specialized computer built specifically for mining Bitcoin.

When it comes to ASIC mining rigs, there are plenty of options to choose from. Some of the most popular manufacturers are Bitmain, Canaan, and MicroBT. The specific model you choose will depend on your budget and goals.

Once you have your mining rig set up, you will need to connect it to a mining pool. Mining pools are groups of miners that work together to mine new blocks and share the rewards evenly. Some of the most popular mining pools are F2Pool, Slush Pool, and AntPool. Each pool has its own fees, payment threshold, and payout system, so be sure to choose one that suits your needs.

Another thing to consider when starting your own mining rig is the cost of electricity. Mining Bitcoin requires a lot of power, which can drive up your energy bills significantly. To maximize profitability, it's important to choose a mining location with low electricity rates.

In conclusion, starting your own Bitcoin mining rig requires a significant upfront investment in hardware and electricity costs. However, if done correctly, mining can be a profitable endeavor that can generate a steady stream of passive income. It's important to research and plan thoroughly before starting your own mining operation to ensure that it is a profitable and worthwhile venture.

THE BEST BITCOIN WALLETS FOR YOUR SMARTPHONE

When it comes to storing your Bitcoin, having a suitable and secure wallet is essential. A smartphone wallet is one of the most convenient options as it allows you to access your funds at any time, with just a few taps on your phone.

Here are some of the best Bitcoin wallets for your smartphone:

1. Coinbase Wallet: Coinbase is one of the most well-known and trusted cryptocurrency exchanges, and its wallet is a popular option for smartphone users. It supports Bitcoin and other popular cryptocurrencies, and it provides 2-factor authentication and biometric login options for added security.

2. Mycelium: Mycelium is a mobile wallet that supports Android and iPhone devices. This wallet is highly secure, and it provides unique features such as local trading, custom transaction fees, and hardware wallet integration.

3. Bread Wallet: Bread Wallet is a simple and easy-to-use Bitcoin wallet that is available for both Android and iOS devices. It supports Bitcoin and Bitcoin Cash, and it doesn't require any personal information or verification for sign-up.

4. Electrum: Electrum is a highly reputed and well-known Bitcoin wallet that is available for desktop and smartphone devices. It supports multiple cryptocurrencies, and it provides customizable transaction fees, cold storage options, and easy seed phrase backup.

5. Edge: Edge is a user-friendly and intuitive Bitcoin wallet that supports multiple cryptocurrencies including Bitcoin and

Ethereum. It provides a Simple Payment Verification (SPV) system that ensures that transactions are validated quickly and securely.

6. Exodus: Exodus is a desktop and mobile wallet that supports Bitcoin and other popular cryptocurrencies. It provides a visually appealing and easy-to-use interface, customizable transaction fees, and real-time exchange rates.

7. Samourai Wallet: Samourai Wallet is a highly secure Bitcoin wallet that is available for Android devices. It provides advanced privacy features such as coinjoin, stealth addresses, and remote SMS commands for added security.

Overall, these are some of the best Bitcoin wallets for your smartphone. When choosing a wallet, it's essential to consider its security features, ease of use, and compatibility with your device. With the right wallet, you can securely store and access your funds while on the go.

HOW TO INCORPORATE BITCOIN INTO YOUR INVESTMENT PORTFOLIO

Bitcoin has emerged as a popular investment choice for investors around the world. One of the biggest advantages of investing in Bitcoin is that it offers a high potential for returns. However, Bitcoin is also a high-risk investment, as the value of the cryptocurrency can be volatile and unpredictable. If you are interested in incorporating Bitcoin into your investment portfolio, here are some tips to help you get started.

1. Understand the risks: It is important to understand that Bitcoin is not regulated by any government or financial institution. This means that there is no safety net for investors if the value of Bitcoin crashes. You need to be prepared to lose money in case the investment does not work out.

2. Set a target allocation: As with traditional investments, it is important to set a target allocation for your Bitcoin investment. This means that you should decide on the percentage of your overall portfolio that you are willing to invest in Bitcoin. Experts typically recommend allocating no more than 5-10% of your investment portfolio to Bitcoin.

3. Choose the right investment method: There are several ways to invest in Bitcoin, including through cryptocurrency exchanges, Bitcoin investment trusts, and Bitcoin futures. Consider your risk appetite, investment objectives, and investment horizon when choosing the right investment method.

4. Consider dollar-cost averaging: Dollar-cost averaging is an investment strategy that involves investing a fixed amount of

money at regular intervals, regardless of the price movement of the asset. This strategy can help you avoid the risk of investing all your money in Bitcoin when the value is at its peak.

5. Stay informed: The value of Bitcoin can be volatile, so it is important to stay informed about the latest news and trends. Follow reputable sources of information, and keep track of the regulatory environment and market sentiment.

6. Consider working with a financial advisor: If you are new to investing in Bitcoin or have limited knowledge of cryptocurrencies, it may be worthwhile to work with a financial advisor who specializes in this area. An advisor can provide personalized advice and guidance on the best investment strategies for your specific needs and risk tolerance.

In conclusion, incorporating Bitcoin into your investment portfolio can offer a high potential for returns, but it is important to be aware of the risks and take a strategic approach to investing. Always do your research and seek professional advice before investing in Bitcoin or any other cryptocurrency.

BITCOIN AND CRYPTOCURRENCY TRADING STRATEGIES: TECHNICAL AND FUNDAMENTAL ANALYSIS

When it comes to trading cryptocurrency, there are two popular methods: technical analysis and fundamental analysis. Technical analysis involves studying charts and market data to predict future price action, while fundamental analysis analyzes news events and the overall economic landscape to anticipate price fluctuations. Here, we'll explore both strategies and their potential applications in Bitcoin trading.

Technical Analysis

Technical analysis is a widely used method for predicting price trends in cryptocurrency and other markets. It assumes that all current and past market information is reflected in the price of an asset, so it's possible to identify patterns and trends that can guide buying and selling decisions.

The basic tools of technical analysis are charts and trend lines, which graphically display the asset's price action over time. Traders who use technical analysis can look for patterns in these charts and interpret them using various technical indicators, such as moving averages, relative strength index (RSI), and MACD.

One common technique is called support and resistance, where traders look for levels at which there is significant buying or selling pressure. A support level is a price point where buyers are expected to enter the market, while a resistance level is a price at which sellers are expected to sell. Technical analysts also use momentum indicators, which measure the speed and direction of price movements, to identify trends and potential reversal points.

Fundamental Analysis

Fundamental analysis involves evaluating the intrinsic value of an asset by analyzing all the factors that could affect its price. For Bitcoin and other cryptocurrencies, these factors could include economic indicators, news events, and regulatory developments.

One popular approach is called the top-down method, where traders start by analyzing the overall economy and then move down to specific market sectors and individual assets. For example, a trader might first analyze the global economy and then narrow their focus to the financial services sector before finally considering Bitcoin as a potential investment.

Another approach is to focus on specific economic indicators that could affect Bitcoin's price, such as GDP growth rates, inflation, and interest rates. Traders who use fundamental analysis can also monitor news events, such as government announcements and policy changes, to anticipate future price fluctuations.

Conclusion

Both technical and fundamental analysis can be useful tools for Bitcoin and cryptocurrency trading. Technical analysis can help traders identify market trends and make well-timed buying and selling decisions, while fundamental analysis can provide insight into the underlying economic factors influencing an asset's price. Ultimately, traders who use both strategies together may be best positioned to make informed, successful trades.

THE BENEFITS OF USING BITCOIN AS A PAYMENT METHOD

Bitcoin, the world's first cryptocurrency, has become increasingly popular over the years, and more and more businesses are starting to accept it as a form of payment. In this chapter, we will explore the benefits of using Bitcoin as a payment method.

1. Lower transaction fees

One of the biggest advantages of using Bitcoin as a payment method is lower transaction fees. When you use credit/debit cards, PayPal or other traditional payment methods, you often have to pay a fee of up to 3% of the total amount. Bitcoin transactions, on the other hand, usually have a much lower fee (1% or less), which makes it a more cost-effective option.

2. No chargebacks

Another benefit of using Bitcoin is that there are no chargebacks. When you receive a payment via credit card or PayPal, the sender can dispute the transaction and have the funds returned to them. This can be a major issue for businesses, especially if it happens frequently. The Bitcoin network, however, is designed in such a way that transactions are irreversible once they are confirmed by the network, which means that chargebacks are not possible.

3. Faster transactions

The Bitcoin network is decentralized, which means that there is no central authority controlling it. As a result, transactions can be processed much faster than traditional payment methods, which can take up to several days to settle. Bitcoin transactions, on the other hand, are usually processed within minutes.

4. Greater security

Bitcoin transactions are highly secure. Each transaction is verified by network nodes through cryptography, which makes it almost impossible to counterfeit or double-spend Bitcoin. Additionally, the use of private keys ensures that only the owner of the Bitcoin wallet can access and spend the funds.

5. Global accessibility

Bitcoin is a truly global currency that can be used anywhere in the world. Unlike traditional payment methods, there are no borders or restrictions, which means that businesses can easily reach international customers without having to worry about exchange rates or other complications.

In conclusion, Bitcoin offers a number of benefits to both businesses and consumers. From lower transaction fees and faster processing times to greater security and global accessibility, Bitcoin is a compelling payment option that is becoming increasingly popular in today's increasingly digital world.

ALTERNATIVE CRYPTOCURRENCIES: THE RISE OF ETHEREUM, LITECOIN, AND RIPPLE

Bitcoin may be the most popular cryptocurrency, but it is not the only one. Over the last few years, we have seen the emergence of a variety of digital currencies, each with its own unique features and use cases. In this chapter, we will explore some of the most popular alternative cryptocurrencies, including Ethereum, Litecoin, and Ripple.

Ethereum

Ethereum is a decentralized, open-source blockchain platform that enables smart contract functionality. Smart contracts are self-executing contracts with the terms of the agreement between buyer and seller being directly written into code. The Ethereum blockchain is designed to facilitate the creation of decentralized applications (dApps) that can execute smart contracts.

Ethereum's native cryptocurrency is Ether (ETH), which is used as a medium of exchange on the Ethereum network. ETH can be used to pay for transaction fees and computational services on the Ethereum network.

Litecoin

Litecoin was created in 2011 by a former Google engineer named Charlie Lee. It is a peer-to-peer cryptocurrency that is based on the Bitcoin protocol but with some key differences. Litecoin was designed to be faster and cheaper to use than Bitcoin, with a higher maximum supply of 84 million coins.

One of the key differences between Litecoin and Bitcoin is the hashing algorithm used to mine coins. Bitcoin uses the SHA-256 algorithm, while Litecoin uses Scrypt, a memory-hard algorithm that is more resistant to ASIC mining. This means that Litecoin can be mined with commodity hardware, making it more accessible to a wider range of individuals.

Ripple

Ripple is a real-time gross settlement system, currency exchange, and remittance network that is built on top of a distributed ledger database called the XRP Ledger. The native cryptocurrency of the Ripple network is XRP, which is used as a bridge currency to facilitate cross-border transactions and currency exchanges.

The Ripple network is designed to be fast and efficient, with transaction times of just a few seconds and low transaction fees. Unlike Bitcoin and Litecoin, Ripple is more centralized, with the majority of XRP controlled by Ripple Labs. However, the company has made efforts to decentralize the network by encouraging third-party developers to build on top of the XRP Ledger.

Conclusion

While Bitcoin may be the most well-known cryptocurrency, it is important to recognize that there are other digital currencies that offer different features and use cases. Ethereum, Litecoin, and Ripple are just a few examples of alternative cryptocurrencies that are worth exploring. As the cryptocurrency ecosystem continues to evolve, we can expect to see the emergence of new digital currencies and use cases.

THE DARK SIDE OF BITCOIN: THE ROLE OF CRYPTOCURRENCIES IN MONEY LAUNDERING

Bitcoin and other cryptocurrencies have been hailed as the future of money, offering the potential for anonymity and decentralization in financial transactions. However, the anonymity and lack of regulation also make them attractive to criminals seeking to launder money obtained through illegal activities.

Money laundering is the process of disguising the proceeds of illegal activities as legitimate funds, making it difficult for law enforcement agencies to trace the origin of the funds. Cryptocurrencies like Bitcoin have become an increasingly popular tool for money laundering due to their relative anonymity and ease of use.

One of the main methods used by criminals to launder money through Bitcoin is called "mixing," "tumbling," or "shuffling." This involves moving funds through multiple wallets or exchanges to make it difficult to trace the original source of the money. Criminals can also use Bitcoin ATMs to convert cash obtained through illegal activities into Bitcoin, which can then be moved to another wallet or exchanged for another cryptocurrency, making it much harder for law enforcement to track.

Another method used by criminals is through the use of "dark web" marketplaces, where illegal drugs, weapons, and other contraband are bought and sold using Bitcoin. The anonymity provided by Bitcoin makes it difficult for law enforcement to track the transactions, allowing criminals to carry out illegal activities without fear of detection.

Unfortunately, the use of Bitcoin for money laundering has led to increased scrutiny and regulation of cryptocurrencies by governments around the world. This has included strict anti-money laundering (AML) and know-your-customer (KYC) regulations, which are intended to make it harder for criminals to use cryptocurrencies to launder funds.

However, some argue that these regulations may stifle innovation and prevent legitimate use of cryptocurrencies for financial transactions. To address these concerns, some experts have called for a balance between enforcing AML/KYC regulations to prevent money laundering while still allowing for innovation and growth in the cryptocurrency industry.

In summary, while the anonymity and lack of regulation in cryptocurrencies like Bitcoin can make them attractive to criminals seeking to launder money, increased government regulations and enforcement can help prevent illegal activities. However, it is important to find a balance between preventing crime and allowing for innovation in the cryptocurrency industry.

ACCEPTING BITCOIN PAYMENTS FOR FREELANCERS AND ONLINE ENTREPRENEURS

In today's world of digital entrepreneurship and freelancing, many people are looking for ways to accept payments from clients across borders without the need for intermediaries. Bitcoin presents a revolutionary solution to this problem, allowing anyone to accept payments from anywhere in the world without the need for a traditional banking system.

If you are a freelancer or online entrepreneur and are considering accepting Bitcoin payments, there are several things you need to know. In this chapter, we will discuss the basics of accepting Bitcoin payments and provide you with a guide on how to get started.

1. Set up a Bitcoin wallet

Before you can start accepting Bitcoin payments, you need to set up a Bitcoin wallet. This is where your Bitcoin transactions will be stored. There are several types of Bitcoin wallets available, including desktop, mobile, hardware, and online wallets. Choose the type of wallet that suits your needs and level of security.

2. Add a payment button to your website

Once you have set up your Bitcoin wallet, you will need to add a Bitcoin payment button to your website. This button will allow your clients to pay you using Bitcoin. You can either design your own payment button or use a pre-designed one from a payment processor.

3. Set a payment amount

Before you add the payment button to your website, you will need to set a payment amount. This can be done in any currency, and the conversion to Bitcoin will be done automatically when the payment is made.

4. Notify clients

After you have added the payment button to your website, you will need to notify your clients that you now accept Bitcoin payments. This can be done through your website, social media, or email.

5. Receive payments and monitor transactions

Once your clients start making payments in Bitcoin, you will receive the payments in your Bitcoin wallet. You can monitor the transactions and keep track of all incoming payments. You can also convert your Bitcoin to fiat currency or hold onto it as an investment.

In conclusion, accepting Bitcoin payments is a simple and effective way for freelancers and online entrepreneurs to receive international payments without the need for intermediaries. Setting up a Bitcoin wallet, adding a payment button to your website, setting a payment amount, notifying clients, and monitoring transactions are the basic steps to get started. With Bitcoin's increasing popularity, it's never been easier to integrate this revolutionary digital currency into your business.

THE FUTURE OF CRYPTOCURRENCIES: FROM BITCOIN TO BLOCKCHAIN-BASED SYSTEMS.

Bitcoin is just one of the numerous cryptocurrencies that use blockchain technology to process transactions. It is, however, the most well-known and has paved the way for other cryptocurrencies to emerge. The hype surrounding cryptocurrencies and blockchain technology has led to the emergence of various types of digital assets that are now available in the market.

One of the most notable types of cryptocurrencies is decentralized finance (DeFi). DeFi is a blockchain-based financial platform that eliminates intermediaries such as banks and financial institutions. It is a permissionless financial system that enables users to access financial services without the need for a third party.

Ethereum is the leading smart contract platform used to create DeFi projects. It enables developers to create decentralized applications (dApps) on its blockchain, allowing for various types of financial transactions and services, such as peer-to-peer lending, stablecoins, and exchange platforms.

Litecoin, on the other hand, is known as the "silver to Bitcoin's gold." Created by Charlie Lee, it uses the same blockchain technology as Bitcoin but with a few improvements, such as faster transaction processing times and lower fees.

Ripple, another leading cryptocurrency, is different from Bitcoin and Litecoin as it does not use blockchain technology. Instead, it uses a distributed ledger technology called the XRP ledger. Ripple's primary use case is its cross-border payment system, which enables speedy and cost-effective international money transfers.

Aside from DeFi and other cryptocurrencies, the future of blockchain technology extends beyond digital assets. Blockchain can play a vital role in different sectors, such as health care, supply chain management, and voting systems, to name a few.

In health care, blockchain can improve data security and streamline data-sharing between health care providers, insurance companies, and patients. In supply chain management, blockchain technology can help track products from their origin to their final destination, allowing for transparency and preventing fraud. In voting systems, blockchain technology can help eliminate fraudulent voting activity and ensure credible voting results.

The emergence of these new and innovative use cases for blockchain technology is a testament to the potential impact it can have in different industries.

In conclusion, the future of cryptocurrencies and blockchain-based systems is exciting and diverse. Bitcoin has paved the way for the emergence of numerous digital assets and decentralized financial platforms. The continued development and expansion of blockchain technology can potentially revolutionize how we interact with each other and different industries.

www.ingramcontent.com/pod-product-compliance
Lightning Source LLC
Chambersburg PA
CBHW071145220526
45467CB00015B/1936